Spilling the Beans on...

Tutankhamen

and other Mummy's boys

First published in 2000 by Miles Kelly Publishing,
Bardfield Centre, Great Bardfield, Essex CM7 4SL

Printed in Italy

Copyright © Miles Kelly Publishing Ltd 2000

ISBN 1-902947-20-7

24681097531

Cover design and illustration: Inc
Layout design: GQ
Art Direction: Clare Sleven

:Spilling the Beans on...
Tutankhamen
and other Mummy's boys

by Martin Oliver

Illustrations   Mike Mosedale

ABOUT THE AUTHOR

Martin Oliver has written over twenty fiction and non-fiction titles for children. He first came face-to-face with Tutankhamen when he was nine years old at an exhibition in London. It was an event that started an interest in all things ancient Egyptian. His ambition is to travel to Egypt. He lives in London with his wife and two children.

CONTENTS

DIGGING UP THE PAST

History lessons are full of kings and queens, aren't they? And all of them dust off the same old mouldy facts about when they lived, who they married and when they died. If only there was some juicy gossip and riveting revelations about them. After all, who wouldn't want to be a king or queen? Surely it must have been great fun to be a member of royalty and enjoy red carpet treatment wherever they went.

Or was it? What was royal life really like? We'll spill the beans on how Tutankhamen and the other pharoahs of ancient Egypt actually lived. Discover the good bits, the bad bits and the downright ugly bits. You'll find out how Tutankhamen came to the throne, how he spent his days, and you'll even have the chance to get under his skin – literally – as we investigate a suspected case of Mummy murder.

While Tutankhamen and the pharoahs are the stars of the ancient world, it would be impossible to spill the beans on their life if it wasn't for the hard work of historians and archaeologists. Films with characters like Indiana Jones make archaeology look incredibly exciting, but the reality is often very different. Most archaeologists spend many frustrating and difficult years working with small clues but just occasionally, years of study and hard work can pay off spectacularly. Nowhere was this more the case than during one hot dusty day in 1922.

Howard Carter was an archaeologist who had been working in the Valley of the Kings for many years. He had already discovered several tombs but all of them had been robbed and were almost empty. However, Carter wasn't going to give up. Years before, a small cup had been found with the name Tutankhamen on it and Carter was sure that the tomb of this little-known pharoah was somewhere in the valley.

His sponsor, Lord Carnarvon, was not an impatient man but even his deep pockets were beginning to reach their limit. Excavating was an expensive business and he had very little to show for his work so far. Carter knew that he was on the verge of running out of funds and was working feverishly..

"Mr Carter, Mr Carter!"

The archaeologist straightened up to trace the source of the call. He saw a crowd of workers running towards him in a cloud of dust.

"What is it?" he asked above the babble of excited voices. "Just one at a time. Talk slowly."

9

His Arabic was not fluent but there was no mistaking the urgency and sign language from the men. He followed them out of the camp and down into the valley. There, in the rocky rubble, they stopped and pointed – to a step.

Carter's heart leapt and he ordered his workers to clear away the rubble. Grabbing a shovel, he joined in and helped them as they uncovered more steps leading to a blocked doorway. With his heart pounding, Carter made a hole in the doorway. Then he noticed something very special on the plaster and stopped. He raced back to his camp and sent a telegram to Lord Carnarvon saying,

TELEGRAM

HAVE MADE A WONDERFUL DISCOVERY STOP A MAGNIFICENT TOMB WITH SEALS INTACT STOP

Carter ordered the tomb to be resealed and posted armed guards beside it. He waited in a fever of excitement and anticipation for Carnarvon's visit. It took almost three weeks for him to make the journey but finally he arrived.

The steps to the tomb were cleared once again and the duo made their way down into the gloom. Aware that nobody had walked this way for millennia, they came to a passageway leading to a door. Carter made a hole into the doorway and held a torch up to the gap.

"Well," hissed Lord Carnarvon. "Can you see anything?"

At last, Carter's eyes grew used to the darkness beyond and his voice trembled as he replied, "Yes, wonderful things."

What they were about to find wasn't just Tutankhamen's final resting place, but a time machine. The journey that the duo had started would take them back over 3000 years to a time when an extraordinary civilization flourished, a time when the pharoahs ruled with absolute power.

A NEW PHAROAH

The dawn sun rose over the horizon, its golden rays glittered on the magnificent River Nile and lit up the bustling brick-built city of Thebes. Despite the early hour, a large crowd had already left the city and made their way to the magnificent Great Temple of Ammun in nearby Karnak. It was the start of the new year and one of the most important days for a long time – the coronation of the new pharoah, Tutankhamen.

The dawn air was heavy with the smell of incense. For many days, priests had been busy sacrificing animals on temple altars and performing other ancient rituals. After a period of great unrest, the court had returned to its traditional capital of Thebes and the temples had been opened again. A great sense of optimism ran through the assembled crowd who hoped that this time would signal a period of peace and wealth. Perhaps the new pharoah, Tutankhamen, would live to a ripe old age and rule over his people wisely.

The prince has already entered a shrine where the blue war crown has been placed on his head. Then he steps out and the high priests place all the crowns of Egypt, one after the other, on his head. The symbols of power, the golden crook and staff, are placed in his hands. At last, he is now the new pharoah.

A hush and an expectant gasp ripples along the huge crowd as the temple gates are thrown open, giving them their first view of their new ruler. Ordinary people, rich courtiers, even the vizier, all bow down before the figure in front of them.

Clad in brilliant, brightly coloured clothes and with the sun glinting off a glittering array of golden jewellery, Tutankhamen appears before his subjects.

The spectators at the back of the crowd crane their necks and narrow their eyes to get a better look at their new ruler. "Is that him?" whispered one. "He's very small."

"Of course," came the reply. "But he is nine years old!"

Long live the King

We are delighted to announce the 100th birthday of our glorious pharoah. A celebration feast will be held at the palace and priests are giving thanks for our beloved ruler at temples throughout the kingdom.

Few people can now remember King Pepy II coming to the throne at the age of nine years but we're delighted to add our best wishes to the longest-reigning pharoah in the history of Egypt and hope that his rule continues for many years to come.

ROYAL REVELATIONS

That's right, at an age when the nearest that most people come to ruling is in maths lessons, Tutankhamen, like Pepy before him, became pharoah of Egypt. And if you're surprised at how young the boy king was when he was crowned, you'd better sit down now. Royal families always seem to produce their fair share of amazing facts and royal revelations – and the pharoahs were no exception. If they had newspapers, this is what they'd say...

THE EGYPTIAN TIMES

Royal Scoop - new King is a Queen.

It's official and you heard it here first - our new king is a queen. A spokesperson for the palace has confirmed that our new ruler is Queen Hatshepsut.

"As the most powerful person in the kingdom," said the spokesperson, "Queen Hatshepsut has decided to bow to the wishes of the people and become pharoah." Despite this break with royal tradition, our new pharaoh is determined to keep up with some well-established customs.

"As all pharoahs are the sons of the god Re, I can confirm that I will wear men's clothes and the ceremonial beard of power. I shall also ensure that whenever my image appears, I shall be painted in male form."

However, rumours have reached us that many people are not happy with our king being a queen. A group of powerful courtiers have made it plain they would prefer a more traditional ruler but will give Hatshepsut a chance.

The Times thinks...
Here at the Egyptian Times, we predict a successful reign for the Queen but don't think that the trend for queenly kings will catch on!

Pharoah Marries - Again!

Sister weds brother

Love is in the air and wedding bells are once again ringing out over the royal palace as King Sneferu announces he is getting married - for the 20th time.
Our marriage correspondent has confirmed that invitations have been sent throughout the kingdom and that the king has decided against a wedding list saying, "I think we've got everything by now."

Breaking news just in:

The pharoah and his favourite wife have just announced a double celebration. In order to keep the royal bloodline pure, their eldest son and daughter will also marry each other.

Minding your P's and K's

The third of a series of tips on correct behaviour by our court etiquette expert:

We have already covered replying to a royal invitation and what to wear — now it is time to deal with addressing the pharaoh. This is a most important subject as calling him by the wrong name can literally mean the difference between life and death.

Calling our ruler 'King' is not only wrong but could be considered an insult that may be punished by the death penalty. Never forget that he is much more than a king, he is a god directly descended from the sun-god, Re.

The correct term that should always be used is 'Pharoah'. This means 'palace' and refers to the fact that the pharoah's body is the earthly house or palace of Re.

DISHING THE DIRT ON DYNASTIES

Tutankhamen's coronation in 1333BC came at around the halfway point in the rule of the pharoahs. One of the most incredible things about the pharoahs is that they were kings of Egypt for so long – around 3000 years. In fact, they ruled for such an amazingly long time that the pyramids, temples and other remains they left behind were considered old even by the ancient Greeks and Romans.

Of course, throughout the thousands of years that the pharoahs were in power, there were hundreds of different rulers. The first true pharoah was a king called Menes. When he came to power, Egypt was split into two different kingdoms. Menes was king of Upper Egypt and in around 3200BC, he conquered Lower Egypt. By joining the two different territories, he created the country known as ancient Egypt.

In addition to this, Menes also founded the first Egyptian dynasty (posh word used to describe a succession of rulers from the same family). It's very difficult to work out the exact dates that individual pharoahs ruled and historians would have been in a fix if it hadn't been for a priest called Manetho.

Did you know? Manetho was the first Ancient Egypt historian. He had the bright idea of writing the first history of Egypt in around 300BC. He recorded the name of each pharoah then grouped each of them into 30 different dynasties – a system still used by modern day Egyptian experts.

THE PHAROAH FAMILY TREE

Thanks to Manetho's hard work, historians have been able to trace Tutankhamen's family tree. The boy king ruled during a period known as the New Kingdom. His predecessors were four kings all called Amenophis but his father, Amenophis IV, changed his name to Akhenaten when he was crowned.

Akhenaten ruled for seventeen years with his principal queen, Nefertiti, but Tutankhamen's mother was another of the pharoah's wives, called Kiya. After his father died, Egypt was ruled by a mysterious king, called Ankhkhprerue Smenkhkaredjerkhepru until Tutankhamen came to the throne. When he was king, Tutankhamen married his half sister, Ankhesenamun.

When Tutankhamen died, there was a danger that the dynasty would die out but it was saved when Tutankhamen's great uncle Ay became pharaoh. However, the only way he could do this was by marrying Tutankhamen's widow, Ankhesenamun – who was his own granddaughter!

THE PHAROAH'S PYRAMID OF POWER

Marrying your own granddaughter might seem like an
extraordinary thing to do but then pharoahs were fairly
extraordinary. The ancient Egyptians believed in a strict social
order in which everyone knew their place. Reaching the
position of pharoah was a bit like climbing to the top of a
pyramid. Once you were at the summit, you literally had the
world at your feet.

PROFILE

Pharoah

STATUS:

son of Re, the sun-god, you are a god in human
form. You are the all-powerful ruler of the country
and as such you are kept away from your subjects,
surrounded by nobles and other influential
advisers.

DISTINGUISHING FEATURES:

easily recognised by the symbols he (or she)
carries, including bull's tail, beard, crook
and staff.

OTHER TITLES:

Chief Priest and Commander of the Armies

JOB DESCRIPTION:

to lead the country, rule the law courts, head the
army and decide trade issues.

QUALIFICATIONS AND TRAINING:

more of a question of being born in the right
family at the right time. However, if you are
particularly ruthless, you could become pharoah
by force.

Vizier

PROFILE

Vizier

STATUS:

second most powerful person in the kingdom.

OTHER TITLES:

Chief Judge.

JOB DESCRIPTION:

to ensure the smooth running of the country. You keep your eye on every department in the government and are in charge of the law courts.

QUALIFICATIONS AND TRAINING:

usually a member of the royal (or a noble) family. Hardworking and hopefully honest. If ambitious, you could be tempted to depose the pharoah.

minister

Ministers and 'King's Friends'

STATUS:

just below the vizier in terms of importance.

JOB TITLES:

ministers have different titles such as Director of Building Works, Keeper of the Crown Jewels and Controller of the State Granaries. Favoured courtiers are friends of the king and have other job titles such as Royal Sandal Carrier and Keeper of the King's Clothes.

JOB DESCRIPTION:

fairly obvious, depending on the job title. However, the Keeper of the Secret of all Royal Sayings isn't a translator but decides who gets to talk to the pharoah.

QUALIFICATIONS AND TRAINING:

once again, it is more a case of who you know than what you know with the best jobs being snaffled by the friends and family of the pharoah.

Nomarch

PROFILE

Nomarchs

STATUS:

nomarchs have little influence in court but are in charge of their own small territories within the kingdom.

JOB DESCRIPTION:

to control their local areas. Must obey the pharoah's orders and be prepared to raise an army if the kingdom is attacked.

QUALIFICATIONS AND TRAINING:

once again, being born in the right family is the most important attribute but influence can be gained through force.

Scribe

Scribes

STATUS:

varied. Status ranges from lowly local letter writer to ministry scribe to Superintendent of Documents at court.

JOB DESCRIPTION:

to learn how to write hieroglyphics and keep written records. Generally it is better not to come up with ideas yourself but to suggest that your best ideas have come from your superior. Accuracy is not vital but keeping your employer happy is. Historical records should always reveal the pharoah as a great ruler and strong commander.

QUALIFICATIONS AND TRAINING:

extreme dedication required. Scribe school is very hard work and children are regularly beaten (so maybe your teachers aren't so bad after all). A strong stomach is required for army scribes, as the most common way to check enemy casualties is by cutting off and counting the right hands of dead soldiers.

Priest

Priests

STATUS:

rises depending on your position within a temple and the popularity of your god.

JOB DESCRIPTION:

there are many tasks within the temples. You may begin by running the temple's workshops and estates before serving the gods direct. Only a favoured few are allowed into the temple that houses the spirit or 'ka' of your god. Followers will leave food and drink for you to give to the god's ka, keeping it alive in the world beyond the grave.

QUALIFICATION AND TRAINING:

many years devoted to one god would normally see you rise through the ranks. Your ultimate goal would be to become high priest.

craftsman

PROFILE

Craftsmen

STATUS:

generally high if your skills are appreciated by wealthy customers, although all villages have their own craftsmen making everyday essentials. In general, your ability will determine your status.

JOB DESCRIPTION:

extremely varied, depending on your craft. Craftsmen include potters and basket makers working for ordinary people. However, special villages are constructed for craftsmen such as painters, sculptors, jewellery makers, stone masons and goldsmiths who are employed by the pharoah.

QUALIFICATION AND TRAINING:

training is often given by being apprenticed to a certain master craftsman and learning is done on the job.

Soldier

Soldiers

STATUS:

depends on when you join up. Until 1600BC
(or thereabouts), the Egyptian army was poorly
equipped with heavy shields, small axes and fairly
useless bows. However, after being defeated by
invaders from neighbouring Hyksos, a
professional army was formed and the status of
soldiers rose.

JOB DESCRIPTION:

varies depending on whether you serve in the
infantry, as a bowman or charioteer. However,
battles are always fought according to strict rules.
An agreed time and place is set when armies fight
each other in daylight on open ground.

QUALIFICATIONS AND TRAINING:

training is given in barracks, then soldiers can
return home unless needed to fight or work for
the pharoah.

31

Peasant

PROFILE

Peasants

STATUS:

lowly.

JOB DESCRIPTION:

to feed yourself and your family, to provide the workforce for the kingdom.

QUALIFICATIONS AND TRAINING:

at this low level, you'll probably learn your skills on the job. Most peasants are farmers who plant wheat and barley and keep birds and a few cattle. Although work is hard, peasants are free men as the only slaves in the kingdom are prisoners of war or convicts.

ALL THE FUN OF THE PHAROAH

So, what would life have been like for Tutankhamen? Being the all-powerful ruler of the country sounds like phantastic phun, but did the boy king have a right royal time or a right rotten time of it? Find out as we spill the beans in our unofficial diary.

MID-MORNING

I am beginning to settle into my new bedroom in the Palace. I had a good night's sleep followed by a great breakfast and I was really looking forward to the day ahead until Uncle Ay appeared. He said that a delegation from Nubia, one of our conquered countries, has arrived in Thebes to pay tribute to me.

I asked Uncle Ay what I should do and he said that we would have to hold a banquet this evening to accept their tributes. He said that he would organise everything and I shouldn't worry. After he had gone, I began to feel a bit hungry. I ordered a snack of my favourite date sweets then I thought I could play a game with my new wife, Ankhesenamun.

MIDDAY ⊙ ————————————

I feel a bit cross with Ankhesenamun. She laughed when she saw me playing with a spinning top and didn't want to play catch so I said she could choose the game she wanted to play. Unfortunately, she loves sennet and so we played that.

Well, all I can say is that Ankhesenamun had all the luck of the dice. I hate that game! Anyway, she was about to beat me when Uncle Ay reappeared and told me that our boat was ready for our hunting. I stopped

playing straightaway and told
Ankhesenamun that we would play
sennet again sometime – but not
for ages.

my drawing – T

LUNCH

...was delicious. My new Chief Steward
is doing a good job. The cooking staff
have finally got the message that I hate
lamb and they brought my favourite

joint of goat instead. Uncle Ay joined us for lunch, saying that his favourite was bread mixed with nuts and spices. After my goat, I polished off a plate of melons and washed it down with some wine.

AFTERNOON ◎

I think that I might have overdone it at lunch. I can't remember anything about our trip to the river. Perhaps the wine wasn't such a good idea.

Still, there was plenty of time to look around as we were rowed towards the marshy hunting area. The Nile was really busy. I saw simple papyrus boats and large wooden vessels, piled high with timber. Along the way, we disturbed some birds from the reeds and we all practised bringing them down with throwsticks. I'm not sure if I hit any of them but my courtiers all said that I was a great hunter – and I smiled in agreement.

Then, at last we spotted our prey – a hippopotamus. It was huge and had the biggest teeth I've ever seen. The beast struggled but eventually our spears found their target. Even when it was wounded, the animal still tried to struggle and almost tipped our boat over. I saw crocodiles swimming towards us and they certainly dined well on the hippopotamus that afternoon. We were all happy at our hunting success and sang all the way back to the palace.

I was feeling very tired after hunting and I really wanted to go to bed but Uncle Ay reminded me of the banquet I had ordered.

I had a good long splash in the bath then my staff dressed me in fresh, clean garments and my symbols of power – what I really hate the most is the ceremonial beard, it always scratches
my chin!

Just then Ankhesenamun came in and massaged oils and perfumes over my neck and shoulders. My wife had really made an effort and was looking a picture in her finest linen clothes. The beautiful gold necklace that I had given her was glittering in the light of the setting sun. To finish off the whole stunning effect, she had put colours all around her eyes, and she was wearing a fresh wig covered with scented beeswax.

EVENING ⊖ _____

The banquet was held in the great hall of the palace and was a great success. My craftsmen have worked really hard over the last few weeks and the gold inlays and bright paints glistened throughout the building. Uncle Ay suggested that I should reward my Steward with a gold necklace – which seems like a good idea.

I could tell that the Nubian ambassadors were impressed when they saw me. I couldn't wait to see what presents they'd brought and I was delighted to receive their gold, ivory and leopard skins.

Best of all, was the latest addition to my menagerie. We already have baboons and an elephant but this new arrival is my favourite. It's huge – taller than three men standing on each other's shoulders – and it has a magnificent neck. When I asked a bit more about the animal, I was told that it eats mainly grass and that it is called a giraffe.

LATE EVENING ⊖

Oh dear, it really is very late – way past my bedtime. Uncle Ay made sure I didn't nod off in front of the guests which is just as well as I was feeling very tired. He mentioned that my ministers would like to talk to me. The Overseer of the Treasury and the Head of Irrigation have urgent matters they wish to discuss.

To be honest, I don't really understand most of the things they talk about so I think I shall let Uncle Ay take care of them instead. Anyway, I have my own plans for tomorrow.

Uncle Ay has suggested that I look into the building of some temples and consider a tomb but I'd much rather go and feed the giraffe.

OFFICIAL DUTIES

Of course, there was a bit more to being pharoah than just hunting and feasting. Nowadays, royal families tend to stick to things like opening supermarkets, bridges and sporting events but which of the following official duties do you think Tutankhamen would have been expected to carry out?

1. Perform religious ceremonies every day

2. Be available to pass laws and judge complaints

3. Show he was fit to rule by finishing a gruelling running race

4. Command the River Nile to flood

Answer: *All of them.*

However, if Tutankhamen was worried about overdoing it, we can spill the beans on how a Pharoah could make light work of his duties.

1. You must make offerings to your fellow gods on a daily basis or the sun won't rise and the world will end. If you're not in the mood or would like a lie-in, the solution is quite simple – just pull rank and ask your priests to do it for you.

2. As leader of the country, you rule the law courts. You are the only person able to pass the death sentence and in theory, all your subjects have the right to appeal personally to you for justice. Once again, a few simple steps will help ease the burden. Firstly, give your vizier responsibility for the courts then ensure your officials keep the public out of hearing distance. If this fails, you could always pretend to be deaf.

3. This is a tough one to avoid but there's no need to worry about fitness training too soon. The running event which marks the end of Heb-seb Festival only takes place once you have been in power for thirty years.

4. This is one duty that you can't really avoid but then this ceremony only takes place once a year. You are expected to

demonstrate your god-like power by starting the flooding of the River Nile to your grateful subjects. This event is vital to the health of your country as the flood waters cover the desert, giving it a top layer of soil and turning it into fertile land for farming. The Nile regularly begins to flood on the 15th July but unfortunately the amount of flooding is sometimes unpredictable – still, even pharoahs can have an off day.

goats-milk shake... fries and cheeseburger...

THE GODS SQUAD

Tutankhamen wouldn't have had to bother about ordinary things like having enough food and money to go around but there was one thing that even the pharoah worried about – keeping the gods happy.

In ancient Egypt, there were lots of different gods who controlled the world and everything that happened in it (a bit like your head teacher, really – only this lot could be even crueller). Priests taught the Egyptian people that anyone who failed to pay their due respects to the gods was in big trouble. If you offended the gods they would not only make your life miserable – they would also turn your afterlife into a not-so-living nightmare.

When your turn came to die, you would face three of the greatest gods in the Hall of Two Truths. The gods would place your heart on one side of a set of scales and place a feather on the other. However, as you might imagine, this was no ordinary feather but was a feather that held all the lies of your life. If your heart outweighed the feather then you would enter Yaru (the Egyptian Afterlife) but if you failed, your heart was thrown to ferocious Devourer and you would be condemned to spend the rest of your afterlife with the souls of other evil, wicked people.

PREMIER LEAGUE GODS

Making sure the gods were happy with you was an expensive and time-consuming business. Keeping up with all of them wouldn't have left you with much time for anything else, so most people chose to worship a few individual gods. As a premier league person, Tutankhamen was probably only interested in keeping the premier league gods on his side. He knew he had to play his cards right.

OSIRIS, THE GOD OF LIFE AND DEATH, RULER OF THE UNDERWORLD
Special duties: teaching people to farm the soil.

ISIS, WIFE OF OSIRIS

Special duties: protecting women and children.

HORUS

Distinguishing features: falcon head.
Special duties: looking after the pharoah.

RE, THE SUN GOD

Distinguishing features: sun head-dress and beard.
Special duties: as the national god of Egypt, Re is
responsible for keeping the nation safe and prosperous.

THOTH, THE GOD OF WISDOM

Distinguishing features: ibis head.

Special duties: invents speech and hieroglyphics.

ANUBIS, THE GOD OF THE DEAD

Distinguishing features: jackal head.

Special duties: decides on your fate during the afterlife.

SEKHMET, THE GODDESS OF WAR

Distinguishing features: lion's head.

Special duties: ensuring success in battles.

SOBEK, THE GOD OF WATER
Distinguishing features: crocodile head.
Special duties: responsible for water supplies to the kingdom.

BAST, GODDESS OF JOY, MUSIC AND DANCING
Distinguishing features: a cat.
Special duties: responsible for fun.

SECOND DIVISION DEMI-GODS

If you were lower down the social scale, your daily concerns would be different to the pharoah's and so would your favourite gods. In the case of these demi-gods, appearances could often be deceptive and some of the strangest-looking ones were thought to be friendly.

Twarat was a huge, pregnant hippopotamus whose appearance was frightening enough to scare away any misfortune during childbirth.

Despite looking like a cobra, Renenutet would help during the harvest.

Of all these demi-gods, Bes was probably the most popular. Despite being a bandy-legged dwarf with the ears, whiskers and tail of a lion, he was believed to protect all members of the family and to keep everyone happy.

WORRY LIKE AN EGYPTIAN

With so many gods in charge of so many different aspects of life, it was no surprise that all Egyptians were superstitious. From the pharoah right down to farm labourer, all ancient

Egyptians believed that dreams could predict what would happen in the future. What do you think each of the following dreams meant?

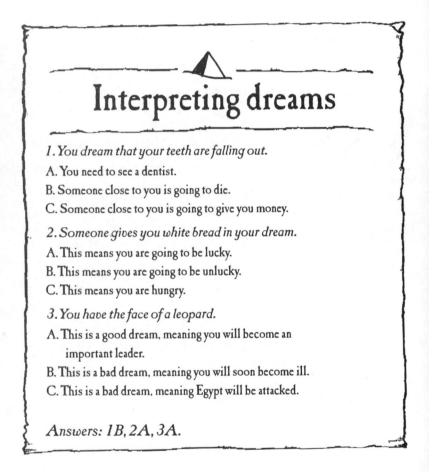

Interpreting dreams

1. You dream that your teeth are falling out.
A. You need to see a dentist.
B. Someone close to you is going to die.
C. Someone close to you is going to give you money.

2. Someone gives you white bread in your dream.
A. This means you are going to be lucky.
B. This means you are going to be unlucky.
C. This means you are hungry.

3. You have the face of a leopard.
A. This is a good dream, meaning you will become an important leader.
B. This is a bad dream, meaning you will soon become ill.
C. This is a bad dream, meaning Egypt will be attacked.

Answers: 1B, 2A, 3A.

As if worrying about dreams wasn't enough, the Egyptians also believed that whole days were unlucky. One of the most dangerous days of the year, worse even than a distant relative's wedding or a French test, was the day of Sekhmet – the goddess who sent diseases.

On unlucky days many people simply stayed indoors to avoid bad luck. Another way to protect yourself was to wear lucky charms or amulets while your friendly neighbourhood priests also offered a solution to bad dreams or other worries – simply place offerings at the appropriate temple. Of course, it was just coincidence that this would also help the priests become richer and more powerful.

DR DO-ALOT

If all your precautions failed and you became ill, you were in with a good chance of getting better. Ancient Egyptian doctors were extraordinarily well-trained and well-equipped. The royal family employed their own specialist physicians for eye problems, stomach disorders – even surgery – while ordinary people could visit doctors at The House of Life, a sort of surgery that was attached to temples.

Many of the remedies prescribed by Egyptian doctors were extraordinarily effective.

From: The House of Life Surgery, Thebes.
Ailment: infected wound.
Treatment: wrap in leaves containing aspirin to help treat pain then powder with copper and sodium salts to dry it out.

Ailment: broken bone
Treatment: set broken bone with cast made from cream and flour. Prescribe rest until healing process is complete.

Ailment: parasitic worm
Treatment: make cut in affected area. Wind stick around worm to remove it then treat with salts to dry the wound. Stitch incision then bind with bandages.

> Ailment: weakness
> Treatment: make up herbal brew of beer, cow's milk and castor oil to build up patient's strength.

However, not all prescriptions were quite so good and some were more a case of kill or cure. Here's one remedy that most people would find hard to swallow.

> Ailment: severe cough
> Treatment: take one dead mouse and swallow whole.

MIGHTY PYRAMIDS

Of course, there was one thing that amulets, prayers and even the best doctors couldn't prevent – death. However, Tutankhamen's predecessors often seemed to have been less worried about dying than making sure they went out in style. Many of them would have made great boy scouts as they lived by the motto 'be prepared'. During their reigns, they spent huge amounts of time (not to mention money) planning and constructing some of the most magnificent tombs ever built – the mighty majestic pyramids.

Everyone has seen photos of the pyramids, someone you know may even have visited them, but how much do you actually know about them? Turn yourself into an expert with our fantastic fact attack.

DID YOU KNOW?

1. A total of 96 pyramids have been discovered in Egypt. They were all built between 2700 and 1640BC.
2. The pyramids were constructed to contain and protect the body of dead pharoahs. Without the body, the pharoah's spirit could not survive but if it was kept safe, the Egyptians believed the power of their ruler would help preserve the kingdom.
3. Three different styles of pyramid were built. The earliest pyramids had flat-topped layers, all built on top of each other. The pyramid built for King Sneferu is a one-off, known as the bent pyramid, while the most common style is called the straight-sided pyramid.
4. All pyramids were constructed on the west bank of the Nile for religious reasons. They were also built on solid rock bases above the flood level for practical reasons.
5. The Great Pyramid of Cheops is the oldest stone-built structure in the world. Its base covers an area the size of eight football pitches.

THE MIGHTY MYSTERIOUS PYRAMIDS

So far, so straightforward – but the more people investigated the mighty pyramids, the more they realised they could be renamed the mighty mysterious pyramids. Despite years of study and hard work from archaeologists and scientists, the pyramids seem to have raised more questions than they have answered. Read on as we lift the lid of the unsolved secrets of the pyramids.

WHY WAS THE PYRAMID SHAPE CHOSEN BY THE PHAROAHS?

Many ingenious explanations have been put forward to answer this question. Some experts think that the pyramids acted like a staircase for the dead pharoah to walk up and meet the sun-god. Other historians have suggested that the shape shows the first part of the earth that rose above waters during creation according to Egyptian myths. Another group has suggested that the pyramid shape was chosen purely for practical reasons – it was strong and long-lasting.

HOW WERE THE PYRAMIDS BUILT?

Once again, nobody really knows. You've probably seen pictures of people dragging huge blocks up ramps of

sand and this may well be how the pyramids were constructed – but no one can prove that this method was definitely used. However, one theory that slaves were used to make the pyramids has been disproved by historians. Records have been discovered showing that skilled pyramid workers were paid partly in garlic and radishes.

 THE MYSTERY OF THE GREAT PYRAMID OF CHEOPS

The greatest pyramid of them all is also the most mysterious. Built by King Cheops, it had stood undisturbed for over three thousand years before another mighty leader, the Caliph of Baghdad, decided to try and enter it. With a little help from a huge army of men, he tunnelled his way through its huge stone blocks. At the centre of the pyramids, he eventually discovered a chamber for Cheops' queen and the king's burial chamber. Inside this huge room was a large coffin. Surrounded by his men, the Caliph watched as the coffin was opened. He ordered his men back and stared at... nothing. The coffin was empty! Nobody else had ever broken into the pyramid, so what had happened to the body of the pharoah? Again, there are many suggestions but no one has come up with the final answer.

A MOST MYSTERIOUS ENCOUNTER

When the Emperor Napoleon visited the same pyramid at the end of the eighteenth century, he also had a most mysterious encounter. After spending some time alone in the king's burial chamber, he reappeared pale and shaking. Later in his life, he mentioned the visit and hinted that he had seen something amazing. When he was dying he seemed to be on the verge of revealing his secret only to stop himself saying that no one would believe him. Shortly afterwards, he died, taking the mystery of his encounter with him.

THE MYSTERIOUS PRESERVING POWER OF THE PYRAMIDS

Many people have noticed the mysterious preserving powers of pyramids. Food seems to stay fresh longer if placed within them and in the 1960s an engineer even sold his patented design of plastic model pyramids as razor blade sharpeners. Once again, nobody seems able to explain these powers.

SPOT THE DIFFERENCE

If the pyramids looked spectacular from the outside, their interiors were just as impressive. In most of the tombs, the pharoah's burial chamber was large and the whole tomb would be richly painted with pictures and hieroglyphics showing the magnificent deeds performed by the pharoah during his life.

However, when Tutankhuman's tomb was opened, it consisted only of a short corridor and four small rooms: the antechamber, the annexe, the burial chamber and the treasury. Even more surprising was the fact that the walls of the burial chamber showed no scenes from the boy king's life – just his funeral and meetings with gods in the afterlife.

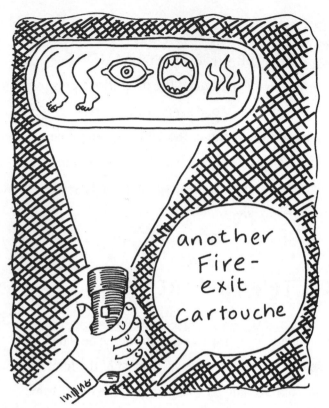

After plenty of head scratching, archaeologists think they may have come up with the answer, but what do you think it is?

1. Tutankhamen had been too poor to afford a grander tomb.
2. A minimalist style of tomb furnishing was in fashion at the time.
3. Tutankhamen had been buried in a tomb that wasn't meant for him.

Answer 3

Archaeologists think that Tutankhamen died before his official tomb could be completed and, as a result, his body was buried in a smaller, private tomb.

The differences between Tutankhamen's tomb and the pyramids don't end there. The pyramids had one large drawback – they acted as a magnet for tomb robbers. It was all very well building a huge tomb and cramming it full of treasures but it was another matter to try and keep it safe.

Tutankhamen's ancestors came up with some ingenious ways to try and stop tomb robbers. Which of the following do you think were used?

1. Building false doors.

2. Killing servants who worked on the tomb.

3. Using huge boulders to block passages.

4. Concealing trapdoors.

Answer: all of them except 2

1. Tomb designers and architects didn't just try building false doors to mislead tomb robbers, they even tried fake corridors and false stairs that lead nowhere.
2. When some of the earliest pharoahs died, their servants were also killed so they could accompany and serve their

masters in the afterlife. (This bloodthirsty practice was soon stopped and models were included in the tomb instead.) There is no evidence that tomb builders and architects were also killed to prevent them stealing from the tomb but if any robbers were caught then they would be put to death.

3. Having placed the pharoah's body and treasures in the tomb, huge rocks and boulders were used to block tunnels and passageways leading to the burial chamber.

4. In an attempt to fool robbers, enormous blocks were placed in front of tomb entrances and plastered over. When robbers uncovered the plaster they would find the block and think it was part of the tomb wall – they wouldn't notice the way into the tomb by the hidden trapdoor above.

PLAN B

The most important difference between Tutankhamen's tomb and his fellow pharoahs' burial places is that his was the only one to survive intact. When all of their best efforts to stop tomb robbing failed, the pharoahs and their courtiers switched to plan B – moving their tombs and hiding them. The place they chose was a narrow valley in a desolate area called The Valley of the Kings. Most of Tutankhamen's predecessors were buried here in tombs cut into the solid rock but even this desperate move only managed to save Tutankhamen's tomb - the rest were all robbed.

It's not hard to understand why tomb robbers thought it was worthwhile risking their lives to steal from the pharoah's tombs, but you might wonder why the pharoahs insisted on being buried with so many rich, valuable items. However, it wasn't a case of showing off, it was all due to religious beliefs.

Like all pharoahs, Tutankhamen believed that the night after his burial, he would make a journey by boat into the

Underworld. The nocturnal trip would lead to him being reborn at dawn with the gods and to ensure he didn't get lost on the route, he could even bring a 'Book of the Dead', a sort of Egyptian A–Z of how to get there safely.

Having arrived, the pharoah could then begin his life in the spirit world and, as a result, his tomb should contain everything he would want in the afterlife. Some of the items

buried with Tutankhamen would be exactly what you'd expect to find:

A throne

Chariots

Hunting statue

Folding bed

His tomb also included some things you might not expect to find:

Model boats

Gilded wooden sled

Writing implements

365 wooden figures of workmen – to work for him during the afterlife

Along with some things you wouldn't WANT to find:

Two mummified babies

Four jars containing the pharoah's internal organs.

Other pharoahs took different things with them.

Which of the following items do you think have been found in tombs?

1. A toilet
2. A kitchen sink
3. Mummified cats and other pets

Answer: 1 and 3 although if kitchen sinks had been invented, they would probably have been included too.

MUMMY MAKING MASTERCLASS

Of course, all these preparations would have been wasted without the one vital ingredient – the body of the pharaoh. As you might imagine, this wasn't just a simple case of putting the dead body into the tomb. The Egyptians believed that the

body had to be preserved so the person's spirit could survive in the afterlife. As a result, embalming became a real skill.

> # WARNING
>
> **this section could seriously damage your appetite. Do not read and digest before digesting your tea.**

WELCOME TO THE MUMMY MAKING MASTERCLASS

The secret to a really professional longer-lasting job is preparation. You will need the following:

1. Premises

It's a good idea to site your business in a tent. This is cooler and lets the breeze waft away the smell of decaying flesh although sweet-smelling perfumes and oils can help too. Call your tent, the 'Beautiful House' – an example of ancient Egyptian humour.

2. Tools

You'll need an array of tools including sharp knives, chisels and iron hooks. Don't forget a state-of-the-art embalming table with a slatted wooden top for easy access to all parts of the body.

3. Workforce

In addition to a strong stomach, a thick skin is required. The people who cut up the pharoah's body are often cursed for injuring him. Keep a look out for potential new recruits as business expands. In the early days, only rich nobles and pharoahs could afford to be mummified but over time, more and more people are being embalmed.

4. Other essentials

Natron – you'll find this salty chemical for embalming around the shores of lakes near Cairo.

Bandages – made of linen, you'll need hundreds of metres of bandages for wrapping bodies.

Canopic jars – small jars that are used to contain the internal organs of the bodies. The jars are sealed with specially carved stoppers, representing four gods who will protect your insides. *Hapy* is an ape-headed god who looks after the lungs, *Duamutef*, a jackal-headed god, who looks after the stomach, *Qebehsanuef* keeps a hawk's eye on your intestines while *Imsety* guards the liver.

You probably can't wait to start but before you begin slicing and dicing, pay attention to our top tip of the day – **MAKE SURE YOU RECEIVE PAYMENT IN ADVANCE!**

Well done. Now you're properly prepared it's time to follow our simple steps to making a perfect mummy.

Step 1   Take body of dead pharoah and transport it to your Beautiful House.

Step 2   Once the body has been undressed, place it on the embalming table and begin by removing the brain (this is usually done by chiselling up through the nose then using a hook to pull out the brain). Then clean the mouth and fill with sweet-smelling oils.

Step 3   Now pack the empty skull with the embalming chemical natron. Add powder to fill the space.

Step 4   It's time for the 'ripper-up embalmer' to do his job. Allow him to cut open the stomach and remove its contents. These are cleaned and washed. Then fill the hole with spices and sew up the body again.

Step 5   Remove all other organs – but leave the heart. This is vital for the king's afterlife.

Step 6   Wash body and cover in natron for forty days.

Step 7   Stuff the body with rags to ensure it keeps its shape. Before winding clean linen rags around it, replace any lost limbs with wooden versions* so the body is complete in the afterlife.

Step 8 Complete the bandaging process, adding lucky charms or gold and jewellery to the mummy.

Step 9 Put the stomach, lungs, intestines and liver in their own canopic jars. Add natron for preservation and seal them.

Step 10 Lastly and most importantly, don't forget to open the mummy's mouth. This is a vital ceremony and will ensure the pharoah can eat, drink and breathe in the afterlife.

* Feel free to replace the eyes with onions or polished black stones

LIFTING THE LID ON TUTANKHAMEN'S COFFIN

So now the pharoah has been mummified, you're ready to put him in his tomb, right?

Wrong. There were still lots of things to do before the body could be buried properly. Until the discovery of Tutankhamen, archaeologists had never found the intact coffin of a pharoah and the amazing finds they uncovered helped to lift the lid on the burial secrets of Tutankhamen.

Before they could reach Tutankhamen's body, archaeologists uncovered three shrines one on top of the other. All the shrines were coated in gold and ornately decorated.

Below the third shrine was a sarcophagus – a stone coffin – carved out of hard rock called quartzite with a yellow painted lid. Within the sarcophagus was another coffin and inside this was another, smaller coffin.

Finally, inside this coffin, archaeologists discovered a mummy wearing a solid gold mask. At last, they had reached Tutankhamen's body.

MUMMY–MANIA

For thousands of years, mummies have fascinated people. Having seen them in museums, in books or on TV, most people think they may know a lot about them – but do they? Why not test someone you know with our true or false quiz...

1. The word 'mummy' is derived from the Arab word meaning 'body'.
2. One king of England thought he would achieve greatness by rubbing powdered mummy on himself.

3. Parts of mummies have been used as medicine.

> ### Take one part of Mummy
> ### 3 times a day

4. The Duke of Hamilton had a strange request in his will. He wanted his hand mummified after his death.

ANSWERS.

1. False.

Mummy actually comes from the Arab word 'mammia' that means bitumen. They were given this name because when some mummies were discovered, they had a dark black appearance and it was wrongly thought they were coated in this tar-like substance.

2. True.

King Charles II thought it a right royal wheeze to rub mummy powder onto his skin.

3. True.

For hundreds of years, doctors prescribed chopped up mummies to cure everything from broken bones to the flu.

4. False.

In fact, the dotty duke decided to have his whole body mummified. His final wish was respected after his death in 1852 and his mummified remains were placed in an Egyptian stone coffin.

UNRAVELLING THE MYSTERIES OF THE MUMMIES

It's thanks to the mummies that historians have been able to spill the beans on some of the lives of the Egyptians.

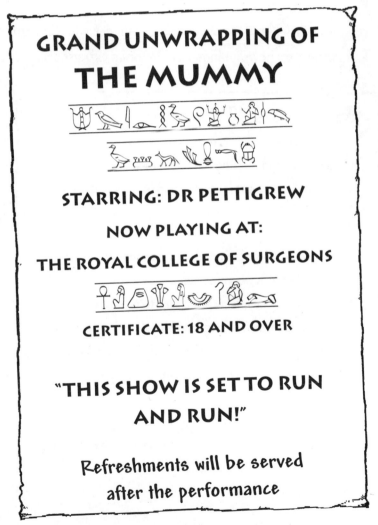

GRAND UNWRAPPING OF

THE MUMMY

STARRING: DR PETTIGREW

NOW PLAYING AT:

THE ROYAL COLLEGE OF SURGEONS

CERTIFICATE: 18 AND OVER

"THIS SHOW IS SET TO RUN AND RUN!"

Refreshments will be served after the performance

The skills of the ancient Egyptian embalmers meant that many bodies were amazingly well preserved and they could be studied thousands of years later. Mummy mania was so high around the turn of the century that unwrapping mummies became more like show business than archaeology.

On one occasion, the members of the audience who came to see Dr Pettigrew's unwrappings were in for an extra shock.

Was it because..?

A. One of the mummies came alive
B. One of the mummies turned out to be a fake
C. One of the mummies turned out to have a wooden leg

Answer: B.

A. There is no record of mummies ever coming to life – except in Hollywood movies.
B. Enterprising Egyptians often used to make fake mummies made from rags and bits of fresh corpses in order to sell them to tourists. It's even been rumoured that the business was so profitable that fake mummy factories operated.
C. The embalmers weren't pulling anyone's leg with this one. If a leg had been lost or had rotted away during embalming, they would often replace it with a wooden limb.

DID YOU KNOW...?

The last unwrapping of a mummy was carried out in 1975 in Manchester. It was the first for over 70 years and was performed by a team of experts using specialist medical equipment to examine the patient... er mummy.

Nowadays, examining a mummy is done in a much more scientific (and to be honest, slightly more dull) way. Mummies aren't unwrapped but are X-rayed or put into a CAT scan. Studies have revealed some fascinating facts about how the ancient Egyptians lived... and died.

Fascinating Fact 1
Archaeologists discovered that most ancient Egyptians had severe teething troubles. The reason was that even though they had over 65 varieties of bread, it was so coarse that it ground their teeth down to their gums.

Fascinating Fact 2
A study of bones revealed that the Egyptians suffered from similar diseases such as arthritis, gout and rheumatism that we do.

Fascinating Fact 3

Pharoah Rameses III was a big leader in more than one way.

His mummy reveals that he was very fat when he died.

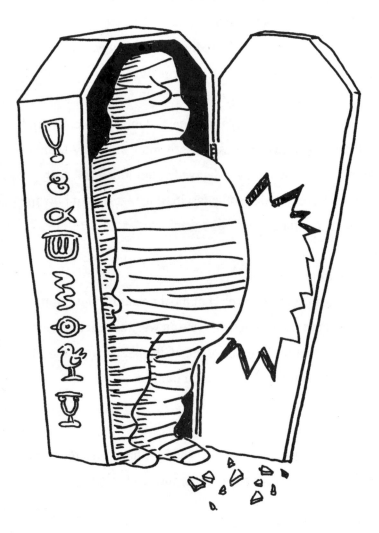

TUTANKHAMEN – A MURDERED MUMMY?

When it came to examining the mummified remains of Tutankhamen, historians were in for a double whammy of surprises. First of all, archaeologists discovered that he was only about nineteen when he died but even more importantly, his skull revealed that he had received a severe blow to the head.

Could Tutankhamen have been killed? Who could have dunnit? It was time to launch a murder enquiry.

Victim's name: Tutankhamen

Cause of death: sudden blow to the head.

Prime suspect: the person who succeeded Tutankhamen to the throne: his uncle Ay.

Motive: if Tutankhamen was murdered, the reasons might lie with his father, Akhenaten.

Akhenaten was an extraordinary pharoah who had the extraordinary idea to do away with all the gods except Aten, the sun-god. To support his religious revolution, he closed the old temples and moved the court to a brand new city in the middle of the desert. This new city was dedicated to Aten and was designed in a completely new style with wide streets and single-storey houses. New styles of painting and sculpting were also introduced.

As you can imagine, these changes had upset quite a few people – in fact, almost everyone in Egyptian society. When Akhenaten died, the mysterious king called Ankhkhprerue Smenkhkaredjerkhepru came to power and continued Akhenaten's revolution.

Throughout this period of change, one figure was present. Tutankhamen's uncle, Ay, was the most senior figure at the royal court. When Akhenaten and his successor died, the dynasty passed into the hands of a nine year old boy – but perhaps real power lay with his uncle.

Certainly, Akenaten's revolution failed. Aten was abandoned and the old temples and gods were worshipped as before. As a boy, Tutankhamen would never have been able to challenge his uncle, but what about as a nineteen year old man? Would he be so keen to listen to good old Uncle Ay? Uncle Ay was used to his position of power and he wouldn't have been so keen to give it up. However, perhaps there was a simple solution – to murder his nephew and take the throne instead.

Evidence: Ay certainly followed Tutankhamen to the throne but did he get his nephew out of the way first? All the sleuthing done by archaeologists is based on a hunch but nothing more. Conclusive proof will probably never be found one way or another so it's up to you to decide if you think the boy king was murdered.

EGYPT-MANIA

The discovery of Tutankhamen's tomb unleashed a severe case of Egypt-mania. Throughout Europe and America, interest in the boy king and his fellow pharoahs became more fashionable than ever before and shows no sign of dying down to this day.

The treasures of Tutankhamen helped archaeologists spill the beans on life during his reign. His tomb helped lift the lid on Egyptian burials and attitudes to the afterlife while examining his mummy may lead to dishing the dirt on a mysterious murder. Tutankhamen hardly made an impact during his short reign but he continues to have a huge impact today and not just because of what was found in his tomb.

The reason for Tutankhamen's continuing popularity lies in the story of the Pharoah's Curse. To get the inside track on the curse, let's step back in time to that moment when Howard Carter and Lord Carnarvon were standing in front of the unopened tomb. Were they about to unleash an ancient curse, a terrible revenge for disturbing the three-thousand-year sleep of a pharoah?

For almost a year after the tomb had been opened, everything seemed normal but then Lord Carnarvon died of an infected mosquito bite and sparked a series of strange stories.

A sudden sandstorm blew up as the last people left the tomb and a hawk – the sign of the pharoahs – was seen hovering in the west.

A physic was quoted as predicting that anyone who entered the tomb would suffer "dire punishment".

On the day of Carnarvon's death, there was a black-out in Cairo and his dog howled then died itself.

For the next two decades, the death of anyone connected with the tomb was reported to be caused by the mummy's curse.

But, if there had been a curse, surely Howard Carter would have been struck down. In fact, he ignored the whole business and got on with archaeology until he was sixty-four when he died of a heart attack.

Yet, some people still can't forget the curse, and in the sixties it hit the headlines once again, when an Egyptian museum keeper dreamt he would die if he allowed Tutankhamen's treasures to leave the country. Unfortunately, the treasures were about to be loaned to France for an exhibition and the keeper's arguments were in vain. After the final meeting, he left the museum, was hit by a car and died within two days.

So what do you think? In the end, the Curse of the Mummy – like the mystery of Tutankhamen's death – is one of the things that no one can dish the dirt on. And yet, perhaps buried beneath the desert sands of Egypt lies another undisturbed tomb just waiting to be discovered and to spill the beans on more secrets of the lives of the pharaohs.

WRITE LIKE AN EGYPTIAN

See if you can write your own secret messages using
these hieroglyphs...

The alphabet:

= A

= B

= C

= D

= E/I

= F

= G

= H

= J

= K

= L

= M

= N

= O

= P

= Q

= R

= S

= T

= U

= V

= W

= X

= Y

= Z

Basic numbers:

= 1

= 10

= 100

= 1,000

= 10,000

other titles in the same series